I Can Read

D0359261

AMAZING SNAKES!

Written by
Sarah L. Thomson

Photographs
provided by the
Wildlife
Conservation
Society

HARPERCOLLINSPUBLISHERS

Dear Parent:
Your child's love of reading starts here!

Every child learns to read in a different way and at his or her own speed. Some go back and forth between reading levels and read favorite books again and again. Others read through each level in order. You can help your young reader improve and become more confident by encouraging his or her own interests and abilities. From books your child reads with you to the first books he or she reads alone, there are I Can Read Books for every stage of reading:

SHARED READING
Basic language, word repetition, and whimsical illustrations, ideal for sharing with your emergent reader

BEGINNING READING
Short sentences, familiar words, and simple concepts for children eager to read on their own

READING WITH HELP
Engaging stories, longer sentences, and language play for developing readers

READING ALONE
Complex plots, challenging vocabulary, and high-interest topics for the independent reader

ADVANCED READING
Short paragraphs, chapters, and exciting themes for the perfect bridge to chapter books

I Can Read Books have introduced children to the joy of reading since 1957. Featuring award-winning authors and illustrators and a fabulous cast of beloved characters, I Can Read Books set the standard for beginning readers.

A lifetime of discovery begins with the magical words **"I Can Read!"**

Visit www.icanread.com for information
on enriching your child's reading experience.

The Wildlife Conservation Society and Snakes

Snakes live everywhere in the world except Antarctica, New Zealand, and Ireland. Scientists from organizations such as the Wildlife Conservation Society (WCS) study wild snakes, along with turtles, crocodiles, alligators, and amphibians. In Venezuela, more than 800 anacondas were captured, marked, and set free so WCS scientists could study them in the wild. WCS scientists found the dens of 200 timber rattlesnakes along the Appalachian Trail in New Jersey, and tracked scores of Gaboon and rhinoceros vipers in the African nation of Cameroon. At WCS's Bronx Zoo in New York, John Behler is the Curator of Amphibians and Reptiles. William Holmstrom, the Collection Manager of the Reptile Department, has studied anacondas in the wild as well as in captivity. To find out more about WCS and the ways that you can help snakes and other endangered animals, visit www.wcs.org.

With gratitude to Peter Hamilton. Special thanks to WCS's William Holmstrom and John Behler, snake experts and consultants. Thanks for photographs to Bill Meng (jacket front flap, title page, pages 4-5, 8, 12-13, 16, 22-23), Julie Maher (pages 6-7, 18 inset), Diane Shapiro (pages 11, 14-15, 18-19, 20-21, 24-25, 26 inset, 26-27, 32), William Holmstrom (pages 28-29, 30), Joshua Krause (page 29 inset), and Dennis DeMello (jacket front).

Library of Congress Cataloging-in-Publication Data
Thomson, Sarah L.
    Amazing snakes! / written by Sarah L. Thomson.— 1st ed.
       p.   cm.— (I can read)
    "Photographs provided by the Wildlife Conservation Society".
    ISBN-10: 0-06-054462-7 — ISBN-13: 978-0-06-054462-1
    ISBN-10: 0-06-054463-5 (lib. bdg.) — ISBN-13: 978-0-06-054463-8 (lib. bdg.)
    ISBN-10: 0-06-054464-3 (pbk.) — ISBN-13: 978-0-06-054464-5 (pbk.)
    1. Snakes—Juvenile literature. I. Wildlife Conservation Society (New York, N.Y.) II. Title. III. Series: I can read book.
QL666.O6T486 2006   2005002661
597.96—dc22   CIP
                                                                                                                                        AC

Snakes don't have arms or legs.

They don't have wings or fins.

But some snakes can climb trees

or swim in water.

Others can dig underground.

Some even jump off branches.

They flatten their bodies

so they fall slowly and land safely.

There are more than 2,000
different kinds of snakes.
Some are shorter than a pencil.
Some are almost as long
as a school bus.

All snakes hunt prey to eat.

(Say it like this: PRAY.)

Some hunt rats or mice or fish.

Many eat other snakes.

A few even hunt crocodiles

or catch birds or bats in the air.

Snakes look for their prey.

They do not have eyelids.

A clear scale covers each eye.

Snakes never blink.

Snakes smell prey with their noses.

They also stick out their tongues

to pick up the smell of prey.

Some snakes can feel heat

from another animal's body.

This helps them

find their prey in the dark.

Some snakes, like boas and pythons,

kill their prey by squeezing.

These snakes are called constrictors.

(Say it like this: con-STRICK-ters.)

A constrictor wraps its long body

tightly around its prey

until the prey stops breathing.

Some snakes, like vipers and cobras,

kill with venom.

(Say it like this: VEN-um.)

These snakes have sharp fangs.

When they bite,

venom flows from the fangs

into the prey's body.

Snakes with venom can kill animals

much larger than they are.

Some can even kill people.

A snake's long, pointed teeth
can catch prey but can't chew it.
Snakes must swallow prey whole.
A snake can open its mouth so wide
that it can swallow something
bigger than its head.

If your mouth and body
were built like a snake's,
you could swallow a watermelon.

Some baby snakes hatch out of eggs.

Others are born live.

Some snakes can give birth to

a hundred babies at once!

Young snakes do not need parents

to take care of them.

They survive on their own,

hunting small prey

like worms, insects, and lizards.

A snake gets bigger every year.
After a while,
its skin gets too small and wears out,
just like your clothes do.
Then the snake must shed its skin.

First it rubs on a tree or a rock
until its skin gets loose.
It wiggles out of the old skin.
A new skin has grown underneath.

Some snakes have skin
the color of grass or sand or dirt.
Others have patterns
that look like leaves.

These colors and patterns
help snakes hide
from animals who hunt them.

A rattlesnake can hide
in sand or leaves.
But if something gets too close,
the rattlesnake shakes its tail.

Rings of thick skin
on the end of the tail
rattle together loudly.
The sound tells everyone
a deadly snake is near.

Snakes can live in trees
or in oceans or underground.
You can find them in jungles
or deserts or your own backyard.

But you're not likely to find

a snake in the snow.

Snakes hibernate in the winter.

(Say it like this: HI-burr-nate.)

They go underground

where they will not freeze.

The snakes do not eat or move.

They wait for spring.

Snakes can live almost anywhere.
But it is hard for them
to live near people.

Houses and buildings
take up the land where snakes live.

Many snakes are hit by cars.

And people often kill snakes
because they are afraid of them.

They don't know how important
snakes are to our world.

Snakes hunt animals like rats
that can spread sickness.
Many other animals,
like hawks and raccoons, eat snakes.

Without snakes,
these animals could not live.
Snake venom can be used in medicine
and may even help cure cancer.

Scientists go into jungles and forests

to count snakes and study them.

Sometimes they put a tiny radio

under a snake's skin.

Then they set the snake free.

The radio sends out signals

that scientists use

to follow the snake.

They learn what the snake eats,

how it hunts, where it sleeps,

and what it needs to survive.

Snakes need a safe place to live
and food to eat, just like people do.
Then they will stay
a part of our world.